Outside the Box

Emery Haley

BookLeaf Publishing

Presentation by *BookLeaf Publishing*

Web: www.bookleafpub.com

E-mail: info@bookleafpub.com

ISBN: 9789357212731

First edition 2023

This collection is dedicated to my beautiful wife, Zoey, who always encourages me to pursue my dreams.

PREFACE

Table of Contents

Who is This Man?

In a swirling fog of gray emotion,
Falling in a pit of chaos endless.
Confusion surrounds me like an ocean.
Will it ever stop to give me recess?

Seconds and minutes and hours and days,
Pass as life continues to parade on.
I search for answers in the things she says,
But words lose meaning in light of things done.

The truth comes out hidden among the lies.
The facts my heart won't let my mind believe.
Silvery words and promises she tries,
But her true affection to I receive?

Hoping for more, I do the best I can.
So this is who I am - Who is this man?

(Non)Binary

Black and White
Dark and Light
Wrong and Right
But what about the gray

Hot and Cold
Young and Old
Meek and Bold
But what about the middle ground

There is so much life
Outside the binary boxes
Beyond the either-or mentality
Lies a world of diverse reality

Gray

In-between
Mysterious and Majestic
Blurring All Shapes and All Lines
Shifts and Swirls
I Am Fog

That Day

I walk in with a false smile
Wish I was bolder
Snip and clip and tip
The weight of hair lifted off my shoulder
I was FREE that day

New confidence – felt older,
stronger, braver, taller,
Free from the lie of “her”
Free to be “me”
Free to be “he”
I was FREE that day

Gender Euphoria

Grand
Emotion
Never
Dying
Endlessly
Restorative

Exciting
Uniquely
Pleasing
Heartwarming
Original
Real
Identity
Affirmation

Brave

People often say
"You're so brave"
"I couldn't do what you do every day"
As if I made a choice to be
The only real version of me
I wish that I could make them see
It's not the compliment they meant it to be
To call me brave would be a lie
I simply chose to give life a try
And not to let my heart's joy die

Community

First they came for the gays
And I marched with Love is Love
Because we are stronger when we march
together
Then they came for the Blacks
And I supported Black Lives Matter
Because we are stronger when we support each
other
Then they came for the abortionists
And I voted for Reproductive Freedom for All
Because we are stronger when we vote together
Then they came for immigrants
And I protested ICE
Because we are stronger when we protest
together
Then they came for the disabled
And I campaigned for Nothing About Us
Without Us
Because we are stronger when we campaign
together
Still they came for me
And an army of "minorities" stood with me
Because we are stronger when we stand together

No More

We light candles
One for each dear soul gone too soon
Light them to remember, to honor, to rebel
against the dark
Until fists and guns and knives stop taking our
lives
Until no more words of hate are weaponized
Until not another trans person dies
Too soon
We hold onto the light
And we continue to fight

A Morning Haiku

Alarm clock buzzes
I arise before the sun
Communing with stars

A Midday Haiku

Working to survive
All day my nose to the grind
Fighting through the day

An Evening Haiku

Sun-down and moon rise
Recharge body, mind, and soul
Time for me at last

Time

Tick Tick Tick Tock Tick Tock Tick Tock,
Click Click Click Click Click Click Click Click,
The hands are creeping slowly around the clock.
Every time I look, they seem to stick.

Why is it when you're excited, time moves fast,
But when you're bored, it creeps so slow?
Why when you want to make every moment last,
Does the clock always say it is time to go?

What is time? We may never understand.
It can't be touched, or heard, or seen at all.
It is everything and nothing, slips through your
hand.
We can't define it, but measure is with a clock
on the wall.

Time is time… or is it more?

Spring

Earth starting to thaw
The days begin to lengthen
Celebrate new life

Summer

Plants green and growing
Animals thrive in the sun
Swim in the Great Lakes

Fall

Birds migrating South
Fallen leaves cover the ground
Bring the harvest in

Winter

Fat snowflakes falling
Lakes begin to freeze
Stay warm by the fire

Twenty-Seven

Twenty-seven is a time of trials and triumphs,
A time of freedom and adventures.
Twenty-seven is a time of fun and energy,
A time of friends.
Twenty-seven is a time of going crazy and
making mistakes,
A time of learning, growing, changing.
Twenty-seven is a time of emotions,
A time of loving and laughing and crying.
Twenty-seven is a time of stress,
A time of being stress-free as well.
Twenty-seven is a time of the present,
A time to live in and enjoy;
Taking the best of the past into a bright future.
Twenty-seven is a time of youth;
A time of crossing new thresholds
Twenty-seven is a glorious fleeting moment in
time,
A time that, right now, is mine!

A Thousand Words

A picture's worth one thousand words,
But I'm not sure that's true.
Just to try and test it out,
I'll write a picture for you.

And when I write this picture,
The colors won't fade with time.
Forever they'll be true and clear,
Because they're held within your mind.

This picture made of words,
Has depth a photo cannot.
It's able to capture emotions,
And show our very thoughts.

This picture is very different.
How very special it will be,
Because all in one picture,
It can tell a whole history.

Of course a photo is faster,
My writing more like a snail,
But when my picture is finished,
It will have the more detail.

And so if you ask me,
"Is the saying true?"
"I would rather have a thousand words,"
Is what I'd say to you.

Dancing

Music has an energy all its own.
It rises and falls, swelling and fading.
Compliment and contrast blend in tone,
Each note like a drop in a pool, ringing.

Notes dance through the air and pull me along.
I lose myself, following their lead,
Moving and twirling held captive by song,
The aching of my feet I do not heed.
I revel in a world composed of sound,
And choose to become one with the music,
A fog of emotion haze surrounds.
I surrender myself to music.

When I have music I'm never alone.
Music is an energy all its own.

To My Airman

All these miles between us,
A long six months apart,
My arms, they long to hold you,
But you're always in my heart.

Phone calls in the darkness,
Soft kisses in my dreams,
But the day I am again with you,
So far away it seems.

I'm hoping and I'm waiting,
To see you home again,
But darling I am with you,
In spirit until then.

Sonnet to Zoey

A light through the fog, a shelter from storms,
Like a rainbow of hope or wishing stars,
Your presence' effect can take many forms,
My strength, comfort, courage is what you are.

I give you clarity, understanding.
My dreams you encourage me to pursue.
Feet firm on the ground, I keep you standing.
I feel loved and secure when I'm with you.

Together we make each other stronger.
Our differences only make us one.
Us, together forever and longer,
Together we have strength not held alone.

Before there was us, there was me, lonely.
Thank you for being my one and only.

www.ingramcontent.com/pod-product-compliance
Lightning Source LLC
Chambersburg PA
CBHW051718130826
49812CB00034B/1237
9789357212731